Recycl

Journeys

Written by Louise Nelson
Designed by Jasmine Pointer

©Published 2022.
BookLife Publishing Ltd.
King's Lynn, Norfolk PE30 4LS

ISBN 978-1-80155-163-2

Recycling Journeys
Written by Louise Nelson. Adapted by William Anthony
Designed by Jasmine Pointer

An Introduction to Accessible Readers...

Our 'really readable' Accessible Readers have been specifically created to support the reading development of young readers with learning differences, such as dyslexia.

Our aim is to share our love of books with children, providing the same learning and developmental opportunities to every child.

INCREASED FONT SIZE AND SPACING improves readability and ensures text feels much less crowded.

OFF-WHITE BACKGROUNDS ON MATTE PAPER improves text contrast and avoids dazzling readers.

SIMPLIFIED PAGE LAYOUT reduces distractions and aids concentration.

CAREFULLY CRAFTED along guidelines set out in the British Dyslexia Association's Dyslexia-Friendly Style Guide.

Images courtesy of Shutterstock.com. Cover – Fotografiche, photka, Tendo, Rawpixel.com, Ton Photographer 4289.
4–5 – vchal, Photographee.eu. 6–7 – Steve Allen, Ann in the uk. 8–9 – Syda Productions, siam.pukkato. 10–11 – MOLPIX,
Vershinin89. 12–13 – Friends Stock, Hunter Bliss Images. 14–15 – photka, Dalibor Danilovic. 16–17 – safakcakir, Hunter Bliss
Images. 18–19 – vchal, Tekkol. 20–21 – Phovoir, rodimov. 22–23 – Anton Kurashenko, Somnuek saelim. 24–25 – Picsfive,
Scisetti Alfio. 26–27 – MOHAMED ABDULRAHEEM, Rawpixel.com. 28–29 – Alba_alioth, Extarz.

Contents

Recycling Journeys

When we throw something away, it goes into landfill. Landfill sites are huge pits where we dump everybody's rubbish. Landfill is not good for our planet.

Instead of throwing something we don't need into landfill, we can usually recycle it. This means turning it into something brand new. Let's look at the recycling journeys of some objects.

The Journey of a Drinks Can

Lots of people love a can of soft drink. Drinks cans are very useful for carrying drinks around. Around 9 billion drinks cans are made in the UK every year.

Drinks cans are made to be used once, then thrown away. This is known as a single-use item. You can't reseal a can and use it for drinks again.

So, what can you do with all these cans? You can put them into a recycling bin! This means they will be sent off to be made into something new.

Once your drinks can is empty, rinse it with water to make sure it is clean and not sticky. Then put it in a recycling bin.

Aluminium cans go to the recycling centre. Then the cans are washed and cut into small pieces. The small pieces are melted down into new metal.

The new metal is shaped and made into new drinks cans. The metal that cans are made from is aluminium. Aluminium can be recycled forever, again and again!

The Journey of a Piece of Paper

Paper is made from trees. Trees are cut down and turned into a sticky, wet pulp. The pulp is dried out in thin sheets and turned into paper.

How many things do you use that are made of paper? Paper is great for drawing or painting on. However, we use it for lots of other things too.

Many paper items cannot be used more than once. This means paper items are single-use items. When you have drawn on your paper or drunk from your paper cup, its job is finished.

When we put paper into landfill, it starts to break down over time. However, when it breaks down, it releases something called methane. This can be bad for the planet.

No need to panic; we can recycle paper too! At a recycling centre, old paper is washed and then made into a watery paste, called pulp.

The pulp is mixed with some new paper, then turned into large, thin sheets. The paper is left to dry, then rolled up. This will then be made into new things.

The Journey of a Glass Jar

Glass jars are useful containers. Maybe you've seen them in the shops, full of jam or marmalade? When they are empty, glass jars can be washed and used again.

If we throw glass into landfill, it will stay there for a very long time because it does not break down easily. Other materials break down more quickly, but glass does not.

However, when you are finally finished with glass jars, they don't need to go to landfill. They can be put into a recycling bin!

When you are finished with your glass jar, you must wash it to remove any food, glue or paint. You should also take off the lid and remove the label.

When the glass has been collected, it is taken to a recycling centre. Glass is sorted by type and colour. Then it is smashed into small pieces.

The smashed glass is melted and new glass is made. This new glass is formed into new bottles, jars and other items, ready to be filled and used again.

The Journey of a Plastic Bottle

Plastic bottles are something we use all the time. They are not heavy, so they are easy to carry around. They are easy to throw away too.

Plastic bottles are another single-use item. Unlike a glass jar, plastic bottles are not made to be used time and time again.

One way that plastic bottles are like glass jars is that they take a very long time to break down. This means we should avoid putting them into landfill.

Luckily, plastic bottles can be given a new life when they are recycled. They can be collected and turned into new plastic, but only a few times.

Once your plastic bottle is empty, you should wash it out to make sure it's clean. When you send it for recycling, it is sorted by colour and then washed.

The plastic is then either cut or melted into small pieces. These small pieces are turned into pellets of new plastic. These are heated up and shaped into new objects.

Index:

Recycling Journeys: Quiz

1. What is a single-use item?

2. How many times can aluminium be recycled?

3. What does paper create when it breaks down in landfill?

4. Can you use the index page to find information about recycling centres?

5. Why is it important to you to recycle?

Helpful Hints for Reading at Home

This 'really readable' Accessible Reader has been carefully written and designed to help children with learning differences whether they are reading in the classroom or at home. However, there are some extra ways in which you can help your child at home.

- Try to provide a quiet space for your child to read, with as few distractions as possible.

- Try to allow your child as much time as they need to decode the letters and words on the page.

- Reading with a learning difference can be frustrating and difficult. Try to let your child take short, managed breaks between reading sessions if they begin to feel frustrated.

- Build your child's confidence with positive praise and encouragement throughout.

- Your child's teacher, as well as many charities, can provide you with lots of tips and techniques to help your child read at home.